BORO SCRIPT MOVEMENT

FREEDOM WORKER

Copyright © Freedom Worker
All Rights Reserved.

This book has been published with all efforts taken to make the material error-free after the consent of the author. However, the author and the publisher do not assume and hereby disclaim any liability to any party for any loss, damage, or disruption caused by errors or omissions, whether such errors or omissions result from negligence, accident, or any other cause.

While every effort has been made to avoid any mistake or omission, this publication is being sold on the condition and understanding that neither the author nor the publishers or printers would be liable in any manner to any person by reason of any mistake or omission in this publication or for any action taken or omitted to be taken or advice rendered or accepted on the basis of this work. For any defect in printing or binding the publishers will be liable only to replace the defective copy by another copy of this work then available.

Contents

CHAPTER ONE

Introduction

Boro,also spelled Bodo,is a Sino-Tibetan group of language, which is spoken primarily by the Boro people living in different parts of India, Nepal and Bangladesh. Bodo language is an official language of the Bodoland Territorial Region of the North East Indian state of Assam. It is also one of the twenty-two scheduled languages listed in the Eighth Schedule of the Constitution of India. Since the year of 1975,the Bodo language has been written using the Devanagari script. It was formerly written by using the Latin and Eastern-Nagari scripts. Some scholars have suggested that the Bodo language used to have its own (now lost) script known as Deodhai.

CHAPTER TWO

History

As a result of the different socio-political awakenings and movements/agitationwhich was launched by the different Boro organisations since the year of 1913, the Bodo language was introduced in 1963 as a medium of instruction in the primary schools in the Boro dominated areas of Assam. Boros are officially identified as "Boro or Boro-Kachari" scheduled tribe (ST) under the constitution of India. Today, the Boro language serves as a medium of instruction up to the secondary level and it is also an associated official language in the state of Assam. Boro language and literature have been offered as a post-graduate course in the University of Guwahati since 1996. There are a large number of Boro books on poetry, drama, short stories, novels, biography, travelogues, children's literature and literary criticism. Though there exists different dialects, the Western Boro dialect Swnabari form used around Kokrajhar district has emerged as the standard.

CHAPTER THREE

Writing system and script movement

It is reported that the Boro and the Dimasa languages used a script called Deodhai which is no longer attested. The Latin script was used for the first time to write down the language, when a prayer book was published in 1843 and then extensively used by Sidney Endle beginning in 1884 and in 1904, when the script was used to teach children. The first use of the Assamese/Bengali script occurred in 1915 (Boroni Fisa o Ayen) and the first magazine, Bibar (1924-1940) was tri-lingual in Boro, Assamese and Bengali, with Boro written in Assamese/Bengali script. In 1952, the Bodo Sahitya Sabha (BSS) decided to use the Assamese script exclusively for the language. In 1963, Boro was introduced in schools as a medium of instruction, in which Assamese script was used. Into the 1960s, the Boro language was predominantly written in Assamese/Bengali script, though the Christian community continued to use Latin script for Boro.The date September 28, 1974 is a remarkable day for Bodosas on this day, as many as 15 people sacrificed their lives for the Roman Script Movement from across the State of Assam. Amlaram Boro and Sibaram Boro of Barpeta, Haitharam Basumatary and

Bisthuram Basumatary of Kokrajhar, Khansai Boro, Kanteswar Boro, Budhbar Boro, Dina Boro and ManshiGoyari of Bijni, Ajendranath Basumatary and NidhiramNarjary of Athgaon, AngelishBaglary of Orang, SombarMochahary of Darrang, Gobinda Narayan Basumatary of Garufela and PhoniramDaimari of RowtaChariali under the present BTR area made the ultimate sacrifice at the hands of Assam Police and miscreants for the Roman script. Since then, in the later years, under the patronage of the Bodo Sahitya Sabha (BSS), Bodos have been observing the day as 'DikharShaan' which means 'Martyrs' Day.' It may be mentioned here that Bodos constitute the second largest community in the North-East Region of India with centuries-old social, political and cultural heritage. The Bodo language is the mother tongue in the Bodo-dominated areas. It is an offshoot of the Sino-Tibetan language family and the first and only scheduled Sino language of the Indian Constitution. Records state that the Bodo-speaking community is well spread throughout Assam, Meghalaya, Tripura, West Bengal, Nagaland, Arunachal Pradesh, Mizoram, Manipur, Bihar and some adjoining parts of Nepal, Bhutan and Bangladesh. The Bodo language has been recognised as the official language of the BTR area and associate official language of the Assam Government since 1984. The Bodo-Kachari kings used the 'Deodhai' scripts to write this language. Cultural icon KalaguruBishnu Prasad Rabha wrote that "the Deodhai script, which is comparable to old Brahmin script specimens is still available in the stone pillar wreckages and main gate to the royal palace of the Kachari kings in Dimapur." However, in the later years, the Bodos used the Roman, Assamese and Devanagiri scripts to write their language. The Roman script was used by the Christian missionaries to write the Bodo language in their religious books towards the last part of the 19th century. When Bodo-medium school education was started in 1963, the Assam Government imposed the Assamese language on the Bodos. However, the Bodos raised their demand for the use of the Roman script. The Bodo Sahitya Sabha in its 15th annual conference held at Khelmati, Sonitpur with a three-day programme from March 15 in 1974, resolved to launch a movement, demanding the use of the Roman script which later became the Roman Script Movement. The movement turned into a vigorous one in September 1974 in which as many as 15 people were killed in police firing at various places across the State. But in the later period, due to the alleged apathy of the Government and the Education department, proper measures for the development of the Roman script were not taken up sincerely. Many Bodo-medium schools have been lying idle while many others are yet to be provincialised. Expressing resentment over the issue, the Bodo Sahitya Sabha said, "For the development of the Bodo language, we have placed demands like special reservation in selection of Bodo-medium school teachers through TET, supply of sufficient books to students, provincialisation of Bodo-medium schools, etc. before the Government, but the Government has totally failed to address our grievances. If our demands are not fulfilled, the supreme sacrifices of the 15 martyrs will not be recognised in a proper sense. So we appeal to the Government to deal with the issue sincerely."

With the Assamese Language Movement in Assam peaking in the 1960s, the Boro community felt threatened and decided to not use the Assamese script. After a series of proposals and expert committees, the Bodo Sahitya Sabha reversed itself in 1970 and unanimously decided to adopt the <u>Latin script</u> for the language in its 11th annual conference. The BSS submitted this demand to the <u>Assam Government</u> in 1971, which was rejected on the grounds that the Latin script was of foreign origin. This instigated a movement for the Latin script which became a part of the movement for a separate state, Udayachal, then led by the Plains Tribe Council of Assam (PTCA). In this context, the Boro leaders were advised by the Prime Minister <u>Indira Gandhi</u> to choose any Indian script other than Latin. In defiance of the Assam Government, the BSSin April 1974 went ahead and published Bithorai, a Boro textbook in Latin script and asked school teachers to follow it.

Retaliating against the unilateral decision, the Assam Government withheld grants to schools using the Latin script. This triggered a phase of active movement that was joined by the All Bodo Students' Union (ABSU) and the Plains Tribal Council of Assam(PTCA). This led to a critical situation in November 1974 when fifteen volunteers of the movement died in a police firing and many others were injured. Unable to resolve the issue, the Assam Government referred the matter to the Union Government. In the discussion, the Union Government suggested <u>Devanagari script</u> as the solution to the problem, which the BSS accepted in the Memorandum of Understanding in April 1975 and adopted later year in the Annual Conference. This ended the Boro Script Movement.

CHAPTER FOUR

Role of BSS

The Bodo people belong to the Tibeto-Burman linguistic family of the Mongolian race. It is widely accepted that the Bodos were the aboriginal or earliest known inhabitants of the Brahmaputra valley. Numerically, the Bodos are the largest tribal group in the entire NorthEastern Region of India and eight largest tribe in India. The Greater Bodo community includesDimasa, Rabha, Deori, Lalung, Tiwa, Madani, Mech, Saraniya, Hojai, Garo, Koch, Chutiya, Sonowal, Moran, Hajong, Tippera, Mahalia, Barman, etc. They are geographically concentrated in different location namely Assam, Arunachal Pradesh, Nagaland, Tripura, Meghalaya, West Bengal, Nepal, Bhutan and Bangladesh. They have their own distinct language, culture and belief system. But the Bodos launched many movements for their justice and to preserve identity in the post-independence period. Among them, the Roman script movement is also most prominent which is first of its kind in the world history in which many innocent Bodo people lost their lives. The Government of Assam refused to recognize the Roman script for the Bodos, but many tribal groups of NorthEast India used the Roman script.

The Bodo belong to the Tibeto-Burman linguistic family of the Mongolian race. Numerically, the Bodos are the largest tribal group in the entire North East and eight largest tribe in India.

BijoyDaimary says that Brian Hodson was the first author to confer the generic name 'Bodo'.

Bodo, however, is an anglicised form of Boro. It is seen that British writers often used the letter 'D' in place of 'R' with strong sound. For example, the word Biri and Kannara are respectively written as Bidi and Kannada in English. Thus, the term Boro(anglicised pronounciation 'Bodo') refers to all the Tibeto-Burman speaking group of Sino-Tibetoorigin.

H.K. Barpujari says that "on the basis of language, it is held that the Bodos, Koches, Rabhas, Lalungs, Hajongs, Chutiyas, Meches, Dhimals and Sonowals of the Brahmaputra valley and North Bengal, the Dimasas of North Cachar Hills, the Tripuris of Tripura and the Garos of Meghalaya belong to the Bodo race. The descendants of the Bodo race in the Brahmaputra Valley and North Cachar Hills, excepting Garos, Koches and the Tripuris are generally known as Kachari." But many of them have of late years become more or less Hinduisedand have lost the use of their mother tongue. It is widely accepted that the Bodos were the aboriginal or earliest known inhabitants of the Brahmaputra valley. The river names of the whole Brahmaputra valley are Bodo namesand it is demonstrable that the Bodos were the aborigines of the valley.The wide extent and long duration of Bodo domination as shown by the frequent occurrence of the prefix di or ti, the Bodo word for water, in the river names of the Brahmaputra valley and the adjoining country to the west e.g. Dibru, Dikhu, Dihing, Dibong, Disang, Diphang, Dimla, etc.They are geographically concentrated in different location namely Assam, Arunachal Pradesh, Nagaland, Tripura,

Meghalaya, West Bengal and in Nepal, Bhutan and Bangladesh. They have their own distinct language, culture and belief system. But the Bodo people in the 20th century faced the crisis of script for their language and literature for which they demanded for recognition of the Roman script. The attachment of the Bodos to the Roman script began in 1884, when Rev. Sidney Endle published his valuable work called "Outline Grammar of the Kachris(Boro) language" as spoken in the District of Darrang written in Roman script.

According to some records available, the then Assam Government said to have introduced Bodo as the medium of instruction from 1904 to 1963, during which Roman was used as the script of this language. However the used of this script was discontinued when in the wake of the swaraj movement, people of India were called upon to boycott the things that were European.

In 2003, Bodo language has been included in the Eighth Schedule of the Indian Constitution. The Bodosare recognized by the constitution of India as the Schedule Tribe of Assam and their language became the 22nd language of India in 2003.

CHAPTER FIVE

How and when the script movement gets started

Scriptis a major characteristic of each developed language in the world. A language is incomplete without a script. The Bodo language has no script of its own.

According to Dr. K. Brahma, the Bodo language "is said to have no inheritd script at present." It is not clear whether the Bodos used independent script in the past.

Bishnu Prasad Rabha, the noted artist, scholar and revolutionist of the Bodo origin of Assamclaims that in the ancient time, a kind of Deodhai script was prevalent among the Kocharis(Boros and Dimasas). Rabha has gathered Deodhai alphabet from an informant of Dimapur area, which was noted for Kochari reign and remains, representing the art and architecture.

Madhu Boro has also written "it is said that the Bodo kings had a kind of Deodhai script, akin to Brahmi, to communicate with neighbouring kings and inscribe on the stone, pillars, monuments, royal gates, stone slates and copper plates, etc. The specimens of this kind of script may be seen till now in an indistinct state on those articles spread in wreckage form in the jungle areas of Khaspur, Maibong and Dimapur,etc". But it is not certain that how and when the Deodhai script was lost by the Bodos. Some scholar believed that they lost the Deodhai script with the fall of their kingdom and discontinued it.Thus, the Bodo people used Assamese script and the Bengali script to write their language and literature.

Towards the end of the nineteenth century, the Christian missionaries tried to write the Bodo language in Roman script, but it remained a limited practice. Later another section is in favour of Deva Nagori script. So, the educated Bodo felt the gravity of the problem while using the different script for the Bodo language and as such, they discussed on the issue in various places and time under different platform and organization for the recognition of one common script which is suitable for the Bodo language and literature. In the meantime, the Bodo Sahitya Sabha was established on 16th November 1952 at Basugaon in the present district of Kokrajhar and whose aims and objectives is to promote the language, literature and culture of the Bodos. Thus, with the establishment of BSS, the highest literary body of the Bodos took the script issue and the script issue has remained a hot debate in every session of the Bodo Sahitya Sabha.

The BSS since its inception faced the problem of using the multiple script for writing the Bodo language and literature. With the introduction of the Bodo language in the primary education, the script problem became more acute than ever before, because the text book in Bodo language had to be produced in one script only. The question of having a common script was discussed inside and outside the forum of the BSS.

According to ManiramMochahari, a founder member of the BSS, the idea of adopting Roman script for the Bodo language was first propagated by few Bodo student and leaders in Shillong. Among them were P.C. Brahma, ManiramMochahari, MugaramMochahari, UttamChand Brahma, J.B. Rajkumar(retired D.C.), J.B. Hagjer(Minister), etc. With the passage of time, this idea gained ground and towards the beginning of the 1960s, it became a general aspiration of the Bodo intellectuals in Assam and elsewhere. The idea was placed before the BSS in its 6th Annual Conference held at Malaguri of Goalpara district on 22nd and 23rd February 1964. Consequently, in the 8th Annual Conference held at Kokrajhar on the 4th to 6th January 1966, the BSS formed an "Expert Committee" to examine the feasibility of Roman script for the Bodo language. The Committee was directed to submit its report before 30th January 1966, on the basis of which acceptance of Roman script was to be finalized. But the Expert Committee which consisted of five members with JogendraKumar Basumatary as the Convenor could not submit the report in time. This resulted to the dissolution of the Expert Committee in the 9th Annual Conference convened at Dudhnoi in March 1968. The executive committee of the Sabha passed the resolution no.11, whereby the Sabha resolved to form a new 'Bodo script sub-committee'. This sub-committee consisted of five members of which SaisingraMochahari was made the Convenor.

Finally, on the recommendation of the Saisingra script Sub-Committee, the BSS in its 11th session at Mahakalguri, West Bengal held on February 24-26, 1970 accepted the Roman script by a formal resolution.

CHAPTER SIX

Report of the script sub-committee

The final sitting of the Bodo script sub-committee was held on the 9th February 1969 at Gauhati. After a long discussion on the matter and examination of the report received from various organization and individuals, the authorized sub-committee has by majority decided in favour of the Roman script on the following consideration.

(1) The Roman script is advantageous for its quick and easy learningand requires only 26(twenty six) letters, whereas there are more than 300(three hundred) letters including compound letters and other variations in Assamese, Bengali or Devnagiri script.

(2) The Roman script is suitable and easy for mechanical manipulation i.e. typing, printing, sending message, etc.

(3) The use of Roman script is commercially economic as it takes less time and labour and it cost less.

(4) It is suitable as medium for writing down scientific subject and technical matters.

(5) It is suitable for maintaining uniformity of spelling and pronunciation among all section of the Bodo people of different places, states and lands using different dialects

and state language.

(6) It better enables to maintain link amongst the Bodo people living in Nepal, Southern Bhutan, East Pakistan and Western Burma.

(7) Further, there is a provision in the Indian Constitution under Article-29 that every language has a right to preserve its own script even Article-343 has also provided the use of the Roman numerals for Hindi language.

CHAPTER SEVEN

Other reason why Bodo people want to use Roman script

Further, there are several reasons why Bodo demand for Roman script for their language and literature. They said that the Kothari Commission had recommended the use of Roman script for the Bodo language. The neighboring Garo people of Goalpara used the Roman script. Famous linguist such as Dr. S.K. Chatterjee and B.Kakoti recommended the Roman script as being the most appropriate for the Bodo language. The Roman script was also widely used in the world.

CHAPTER EIGHT

Roman script implementation sub-committee

The report of the script sub-committee was discussed in the 11th Annual conference held on the 24th to 26th February 1970 at Mahakalguri of West Bengal wherein the Sabha resolved its decision to adopt the Roman script. In the same conference the Sabha formed the 'Roman script implementation sub-committee' with KanakeswarNarzary and Thaneswar Boro as convenor and chairman respectively. This sub-committee had three consecutive sittings. The report of the implementation sub-committee suggested the BSS to initiate the implementation by publishing all the official circulars and pamphlets in Roman script. The report also suggested arranging seminars and free classes to familiarize the Roman script mainly with the Bodo teachers, the L.P. and M.E. school children and the old batch of Bodo writers. The Sub-Committee also advised the BSS to appeal the authorized writers to convert their text books into Roman script and to approach the Commission for Minority Language of India to sanction grants for holding seminars and classes. The sub-committee also suggested the Sabha to approach Assam Government for the approval of the text books written in Roman script. The sub-committee suggested the BSS to introduce the Bodo Text Books in Roman script from class I in the primary stage step by step starting right from the academic year of the 1971.

However, the official record of the BSS shows that the Sabha could not materialize its decision of implementing the Roman script from the academic session of 1971.These enable the BSS to resume the Roman script issue. The Sabha in its 15th Annual Conference convened at Khelmati near Tezpur on the 17th and 18th March 1974 resolved to implement Roman script and decided to implement the Bodo Primer 'Bithorai' in Roman script in class I of Bodo medium primary schools from the academic year 1974. To materialize this decision, the Sabha organized an inaugural ceremony on the 22nd April 1974 in which the Roman script was declared as the common script for the Bodo language and literature throughout Assam and outside and openly declared Sabha's decision to introduce Bithorai(Balab-Se), the Bodo Primer written in Roman script. The General Secretary of the BSS appeal to all the teachers of Bodo medium primary school to introduce the above mentioned Bodo Primer in class I.

CHAPTER NINE

Entry of Assam Government in the script movement

The introduction of the Bodo Primer Bithorai without the prior approval of the authority concerned ultimately brought the Government of Assam in the scene. The Government as an act of disapproval ordered to stop the payment of the Bodo medium primary school teachers of those schools where Roman script was found being introduced. Orders were also issued to stop the grants of those schools. Consequently, payment and grants of those teachers and schools were stop from June 1974. The deputation consisting of 26 representatives of the NalbariDistrict Primary Bodo Teacher's Association when enquired in the Regional Board for Elementary Education, Nalbari on the 16th July 1974 was told that such measure was taken as per the order of the Government of Assam.

CHAPTER TEN

Different phases of the Mass Movement

Assam Government decision to stop the payment of the Bodo Medium Primary school teachers and the grants of Bodo Medium schools brought an abrupt change in the situation. In consequence, the BSS launched a full-scale movement demanding Government's recognition of the Roman script for the Bodo language and literature and withdrawal of Government's action against the teachers of the Bodo medium schools. It was a mass movement being participated by the entire Bodo including the organizations like PTCA and ABSU. There were continuous bandhs and boycott of schools and colleges for several months in the Bodo dominated areas. Later on, the movement turned into violent and 15 Bodo agitators died in police firing and considerable property was lost in arson and other types of violent attacks. The Sabha received wide response from the Bodo masses as a result of which in the first and second phases of the movement, the Bodo students were found abstaining from their classes and demonstrating in front of Sub-Division and District Offices.

At the end of the second phase, the movement was called off temporarily. This was done in response to the appeal made by the Bodo minister and MLAs in whose meditation a joint memorandum of the Bodo minister, Bodo MLAs and the BSS was submitted to the chief minister Sarat Chandra Sinha on 24th December 1974. This however did not receive favourable response from the Government. As a result, the BSS was forced to resume the third phase of its movement from the 27th September 1974.

The third phase which lasted till the 28th November 1974 had proved to be the most spirited and significant in the history of the Bodo script movement. The Bodo volunteers were seen coming out in thousand and demonstrating in front of the sub-divisional and district head offices. Incidents of police firing first took place in the district of Goalpara, where on the 18th and 19th November 1974, six Bodo volunteers and two CRPF were killed. The official report noted "police fired to disperse about 10,000 armed tribal who stormed the sub-deputy collector's office at Bijni present Chirang district" and the disturbance spread to Kokrajhar and Gossaigaontownship of the district when about 15,000 tribal armed with lethal weapons demonstrated in front of the office of the sub-deputy collectors and block development offices.Udalguri in the district of Darrang, one person was killed as a result of police firing and on the 25th November 1974, more than six hundred Bodo volunteers were arrested. At Tangla, Rowta and other adjoining areas situation remained tense while at Rangia police resorted to lathi charge.

The BSS version gives different account of the report that the Bodo volunteers were equipped with lethal weapons. In the press statement, the BSS president noted that on the 18th November 1974, around 3000 Bodo volunteers were demonstrating peacefully in front of the Sidli sub-deputy collector's office. A band of CRPF chased them, also open fired at them from their guns. Narrating the incident of Bijni which took place on the 19th November 1974, the president says that around 10,000 demonstrators gathered in front of the sub-deputy collector's office. According to the report furnished by the observer of the BSS, the picketers did not carry any lethal weapons except foster and placards. Basing on the report of the BSS's observer, the president argued that if 10,000 volunteers were really equipped with lethal weapons only seven CRPF would have not been injured. Another argument of the president was that among the picketers, there was a big number of women and in their presence, the male picketers would not take the risk of confronting with the CRPF. According to BSS observer, the CRPF open fired on a crowd of ten thousand picketers resulting stamped in which seven CRPFs were injured. On that particular day, 3 volunteers were killed in police firing and more than ten were injured.

When the movement was on its zenith, the Assam Government appealed to the BSS to sit for a negotiation. The BSS with a hope solving the problem on the table accepted the Government's call for a talk. As a result, talk between the education minister HarendraNathTalukdar and ten representatives of the Sabha were held on the 28th November 1974. In the talk, the education minister failed to bring amicable solution to the problem. The Government of Assam sensed a separatist tendency in the move and refused the demand of the BSS. The dominant Assamese elite and the AsomSahitya Sabha, the prominent literary organization of Assam also opposed the move having seen anti-Assamese feeling in it.The other reason why Government refused to concede the demand for Roman script perhaps mainly because a misconception is widely prevalent in the Government circles that a demand for

Roman script always arises out of pro-Christian Missionary and anti-Indian attitudes.

CHAPTER ELEVEN

Intervention of Central Government

Finally the SaratCh. Sinha- led Government of Assam referred the matter to the Central Government in New Delhi. Meanwhile the State of Emergency was proclaimed throughout the country by Indira Gandhi led Congress Government in 1975. The Central Government utilized the threat of emergency provisions of arrest and detention to force the Bodo leaders to accept Devnagiri script for the Bodo language. The Central Government had been suggesting Dharanidhar Basumatary, the lone MP of the Bodo community and Prime Minister Smt. Indira Gandhi herself advised the BSS representatives to adopt Devnagiri script for their language and literature. The BSS in its talk in Delhi could not persuade the centre to change its decision. Finally, the BSS fell between the unyielding attitudes of the State and Central Government. But ultimately on the 9th April 1975, the two BSS representatives Ramdas Basumatary and Thaneswar Boro prepare proposal in favour of Devnagari script and submitted to the Prime Minister of India. This proposal, they prepared during their stay in Delhi and had no prior consent of the other members of the Sabha. The proposal also contained in it a complete scheme for the implementation of the Devnagiri script. The BSS officially accepted the Devnagiri script in its 16th Annual Conference convened at Dhing on the 25th to 27th April 1975. The Sabha took this decision to give 'more wightage to the perspective of national integration and wider cultural contact'. It however added that the BSS would revert to its original stand for Roman script if the centre did not implement other conditions place by the Sabha.

CHAPTER TWELVE

Reaction for the acceptance of Devnagiri script

With this the Bodo movement for the Roman script ended without achieving its desired goal. This benefited neither the Government nor the Bodo people. The acceptance of Devnagari script caused reaction among the many Bodos and Ramdas Basumatary and Thaneswar Boro were accused. Many of them were found raising voice of protest against this decision of the BSS. The Bodo students found the Devanagari script a totally unfamiliar script to them andalso much more difficult to master than the more familiar Assamese script. The replacement fuelled the anti-Assamese attitude of the Bodo educated youth. Even in the face of sufferings and atrocities, the Bodo masses remained firm of their caused. As a result, BSS's decision to accept Devnagiri script was looked down upon as an act of treachery. B.N. Brahma, an advocate from Dhubri in his letter to The Assam Tribune accused the two representatives of Bodo Sahitya Sabha of taking arbitrary decision and appealed them to collect opinions from people before implementation. Sukaram Basumatary, Malati Basumatary and BirendraNath Brahma in their letter to 'The Assam Tribune' blamed the two BSS members who took part in the discussion in Delhi. According to them 'the two-men BSS delegation unhesitatingly accepted Devnagiri script as alternative to Roman'. A section of the Assamese intellectual also spoke out against the acceptance of the Roman script and advised to go back to the Assemese script.

CHAPTER THIRTEEN

Repeat of script issue

A small section of the Bodos is still advocating for the Roman script for Bodo language. It was in 1987, the issue of script was reopened by ABSU President Upendranath Brahma in his charter of 92 demands in which the memorandum was submitted to the Governor of Assam. In 1993, with formation of Bodoland Autonomous Council (BAC), Roman script was once again implemented for the Bodo language and literature. Though this time the Assam Government has recognized the Roman script for the Bodos but problem arouse within the Bodo community itself because some advocate for Roman script and some favour for Devnagiri script. This resulted as SatyendraNathMondal observes that a number of tragic incidents took place and many valuable lives were lost over the script issue. Such incident among the Bodos indicates that the Bodos were not unanimous in their acceptance of either the Devnagiri or the Roman script. But the prolonged use of the Devnagiri script in all matters of communication became gradually convenient for the Bodo people to accept the script in their language. In the 39th session of the BSS held at Kokrajhar on March 2000, Devnagiri was accepted unanimously (except NDFB). But it is unfortunate that the NDFB shot dead the president of BSS Bineswar Brahma on

August 19, 2000 and Brahma was shot dead by the outfit on suspicion that he had advocated the use of Devnagiri script for the Bodo language while the NDFB has been demanding for the Roman script. The chairman of the outfit had threatened to kill Sri Brahma if he failed to accept Roman script for the Bodo language in a meeting held in Shillong on May 30, 1999. Above all, the BSS felt that in the interest of the integration of the nation it would be more pertinent to include Devnagiri script.In fact the Devnagiri script has become an inseparable part in the development of the Bodo language and literature and change of the script may relapse the whole intellectual process of the Bodos. But the script issue has remained as a vexed problem in spite of the acceptance of the Devnagiri script due to anomaly in using script for writing Bodo language.

CHAPTER FOURTEEN

Causes of the failure of script movement

A review of the facts and events of the Bodo movement of the Roman script show that the Bodos were the victims of some of the leaders of their own. Looking at the systematic programmes and the intensity of the movement, one will readily able to say that the lack of leadership to be the only cause behind its failure. According to the opinions of the others BSS members, the proposal submitted to the Prime Minister was not prepared by the central executive committee nor were the two representatives authorized to do so. Their switching over from Roman to Devnagiri script showed the lack of strong determination in their part. It is true that BSS was place in a deplorable condition with the Assam Government unwilling to solve the problem and the centre trying to persuade it to accept Devnagiri script. However had there been able leadership and strong determination, the BSS could pull even through such situations.

Another major factor that largely contributed to the failure of Bodo movement for Roman script appears to be the strong opposition raised by a section of the Assamese intellectuals. This section of the Assamese intellectuals wanted the Bodos to continue with the Assamese script. Mention has been already made that the Assam Sahitya Sabha (ASS) could not come to a consensus with the BSS in regard to the script issue. The writers conference organized by the Assam Sahitya Sabha from the 6th to 9th November 1974 where the question of Roman script issue was discussed ended with the suggestion that "for cultural integration and development of tribal language in the state, Assamese script is enough and suitable". Many of the Assamese intellectual put separatist colour on the Roman script movement and suspected hands of foreign missionaries behind it. A 'Special Representatives' while writing on the Bodo script movement in the SaptahikNilachal noted the movement to be "a manifestation of a strong anti-Assamese feeling" and related it to the Udayachal demand of the Plain Tribal Council of Assam (PTCA)saying them to be "the two sides of same coin". Few of the Assamese intellectuals were opposed to the introduction of Devnagiri script too. In Baganpara, the school inspector H.Ahmed was found issuing Bodo text books written in Assamese script even long after the order of implementation of the Devnagiri script. Such an opposition of the Assamese intellectual who dominated almost all the institutions in the state must have created a situation where the SaratSinha Government found it difficult to take a decision of its own. The argument of the Assam Sahitya Sabha that the adoption of the Roman script by the Bodos would bring cultural disintegrity and communal disharmony in the state of Assam appears to be a one sided view. The Assamese idea of maintaining integrity of the state by using one script may not be practicable in a democratic country like India where constitutional safeguard are given for the culture and language of different ethnic groups. In any case, integrity of the state or of a nation cannot be confirmed to the use of one script or one language. Especially in India, where various ethnic groups with different culture and language are found, the integrity was to be a composite whole of all the diversities of the different communities. Otherwise, integrity of India or any of the state may mean culture domination of one on the other. In that case, there are more chances of once being alienated by the other, which ultimately may lead to socio-political unrest, shaking the very idea of integrity of a state or of a nation.

Added to these was the unyielding attitude of the Assam Government that contributed to the failure of the Roman script movement of the Bodos. It is true that in the wake of script movement the Assam Government fell under the sphere of three opposing forces- the Bodos demanding Roman script, the Assamese intellectual pressing hard for the continuation of Assamese script and the centre trying to champion for national integrity by introducing Devnagiri script. But perhaps a strong state Government could have solved the script problem in the state level itself. PitsingKonwar, an MLA, while discussing the Roman script issue in the Assembly urged the state Government not to allow the Central Government to interfere in the matter of language which was a state subject. But the Sinha Government could not solve the script problem without necessary directions from the centre.

CHAPTER FIFTEEN

Impact of the script movement

The Roman script movement which was launched by the Bodo Sahitya Sabha (BSS) in 1974 involved the whole of Bodo community all over the region of Assam followed by massive police operations in all the Bodo-dominated areas resulting in untold miseries of the people. During the period of the Roman script movement, all the prominent leaders belonging to the Bodo community had to go underground in order to evade repressive police actions. Many of the leaders of the BSS and the PTCA were arrested by the Assam Police and put behind the bar. A reign of terror was let loose by the Assam Home Minister Shri HiteshwarSaikia and several valuable lives were lost in the unprovoked police firings. Clandestinely, it was learnt from some unidentified well-wisher that there was a secret instruction to the police to eliminate some of the top Bodo leader for their role in the Roman script movement which ended just little before the proclamation of the National Emergency by Indira Gandhi led Congress Government at the Centre in 1975. A section of the Assamese people also opposed the Bodo demand and at many times they beaten up the inmates in the houses as if they were the police personnel. These hurt the hearts of the Bodo people which widened the little gap already created between the two groups of people. The later course of events showed that the Bodo people could never forget and forgive the treacherous acts of the Assamese people and choose to separate out of Assam itself. They became conscious of their own identity and began to claim it to be separate from Assamese mainstream. So, many a time the use of Devnagiri script creates a communication gap in between the old intellectuals and the newly educated ones due to their knowledge of two different scripts. Thus, it is clear thatduring this period the Bodo literature face tough situations which slow down its growth.

CHAPTER SIXTEEN

Conclusion

The Roman script movement of 1974-1975 is the first of its kind in the history of the Bodos as well as in the world propagated by a small group of Bodo students and leaders of Shillong. The idea of adopting Roman script spread among the Bodo intellectuals and with the acceptance of it by the BSS, the script issue involved the whole of Bodo community. The Bodo script movement is one of the longest movements of the Bodo Sahitya Sabha. The script movement is quite well-organized both from the structural and functional points of view. The intensity of the movement engulphed almost every corner of the Bodo populated areas and in the course of the movement as many as 15 volunteers sacrificed their lives, to whom the BSS consider as "Roman script Martyrs". There is one village in Kokrajhar district near Kokrajhar town whose name is Romanpara given after the cremation of two volunteer in that place who were shot dead by the Assam Police. It is observed that the main cause of the failure of the Roman script movement was the lack of leadership which was accelerated by the opposition of the Assamese intellectuals and by the unyielding attitude of the Assam Government. The Roman script movement has clear cut cultural overtones both in terms of its declared goal and in terms of the efforts of the Bodo Sahitya Sabha to preserve, revive and develop Bodo literature and other aspects of their culture. At present, the Bodo people are using the Devnagiri script for their language and literature and are working for its all round development.

CHAPTER SEVENTEEN

Final Acceptance of Devanagari script

The Devanagari script for Boro language was an unexpected development and it was not immediately accepted by the wider group of Boro community. The BSS too failed to implement the use of the Devanagari script and some of the writers continued to use the Assamese/ Bengali and Latin scripts. In 1982, the All Bodo Students Union (ABSU) included the demand of the Latin script in Boro medium schools in its charter of Demands. Following an expert committee report constituted by the BSS, the Bodoland Autonomous Council (BAC) adopted a resolution to use Latin script in its territory which the Assam Government too accepted.

Nevertheless, in the discussion with the Bodo Liberation Tigers (BLT), the Government of India (GoI) demanded the implementation of the earlier agreement with the BSS on the use of the Devanagari script if the Boro language was to be included in the Eighth Schedule of the Indian Constitution. Following this, the ABSU and the BSS agreed to use the Devanagari script exclusively and the matter was finally settled.